INSPIRED CRICKET
PRACTISE LIKE THE PROS

Published by Inspired Sports Publishing, 2009
Copyright © Iain Brunnschweiler 2009

No reproduction without permission

INSPIRED CRICKET
PRACTISE LIKE THE PROS

"In memory of Terry Trodd, a man who's passion and enthusiasm for cricket had such an effect on so many young players."

ACKNOWLEDGEMENTS

I would like to thank every cricket player and coach that I have come into contact with over the last 16 years, ever since I learned that there was a game called cricket. It is such an unusual and interesting game and absolutely everyone has an opinion or an idea about how it should be played, which has meant that I have picked the brains of hundreds, perhaps thousands, of individuals.

Most of the drills and games in this manual have been passed down from coach to coach, and player to player, and adapted along the way. I thank everyone for their thoughts and ideas over the years.

Thanks to Matt and Mark at TriNorth for all of their work and input into the process.

Thanks to all of the players who have contributed quotes – hopefully your words will help the next generation of international cricketers!

Thanks to Rick for making this dream a reality.

Finally I'd like to thank my family for their endless support, and to Justine for putting up with me even though she's not a cricket fan!

Be inspired.

Brunchy.

CONTENTS

8 Introduction to Inspired Cricket
11 KP's Approach to Cricket
12 Warm-ups
32 Fielding – Agility
40 Fielding – Throwing-based drills
52 Fielding – Catching-based drills
68 Net Practice – Introduction
70 Net Practice – Batsmen
78 Net Practice – Bowlers
82 Wicket-keeping

INTRODUCTION

INSPIRED CRICKET

Welcome to Inspired Cricket!

The aim of this manual is to act as a resource for coaches and players, so that they can get the most benefit out of every single practice session, and be inspired to make sure that everyone involved enjoys themselves. If set up and run in the right way, the same drills, games and challenges can be used to work with under 9s who have never played before, all the way through to full-time professional cricketers.

Inspired Cricket is all about creating an 'EPIC' learning environment, that is:

◀ **ENJOYABLE** ▶

◀ **PROGRESSIVE** ▶

◀ **INNOVATIVE** ▶

◀ **CHALLENGING** ▶

PRO TIP

Iain Brunnschweiler
"Having worked regularly with pros, club cricketers and juniors, I have found that ulitmately they are all just kids at heart, and want to enjoy what they are doing! I often use the same drills with pros and club juniors, you just have to set them up and make sure everyone is getting something out of it and having fun. I try to be inspired to vary the drills and games to keep everyone interested."

ABOUT THE AUTHOR

Iain Brunnschweiler is a full-time member of the coaching staff at Hampshire CCC working with the professionals and academy players, and is also club coach of Burridge CC. He is currently in the ECB Elite coaching programme working towards his Level 4 qualification, and has a degree in Sport and Exercise Science. He completed his dissertation in the biomechanics of fast bowling, which he presented at the BASES Annual student conference.

He was a professional on the staff at Hampshire from 2000-2003, making his Championship debut against Yorkshire at Scarborough, and his one-day debut against Middlesex at The Rose Bowl. He also represented England at under 17 level, playing in an International Youth Tournament in Bermuda in 1997.

His career highlight in cricket was hitting the winning runs against Steve Waugh's all-conquering Australians in 2001 during a tour match at the Rose Bowl. His other notable sporting achievement was representing AFC Totton at the new Wembley in May 2007 in the FA Vase Final, in front of a crowd of 35,000.

INTRODUCTION

THE CONCEPT

The role of the cricket coach is a challenging one, whether trying to work with the under 9s, or trying to encourage the 20-season veterans to engage themselves in training in an enjoyable and productive manner. Inspired Cricket is a manual which aims to open up the mind of the club coach to interesting and innovative drills, games and challenges to try to increase interest and add variation to the traditional club 'nets' or practice nights.

Inspired Cricket covers a range of topics – from warm-ups and fielding drills, through a range of different ways to approach net practice to make it more challenging and game-based, to a section for the much-overlooked wicket-keepers, who play such a vital role in team dynamics.

As a coach working with players, all you need to do is pitch the challenge of the drill at the same level as the players you are working with. If you make it too hard – or too easy – your players will lose interest, so the skill is to work out the correct level for your group or individual. Just like any skill, this gets easier with practice. Whether you are a player or a coach, the message is simple……

Get out there and try things, learn from your mistakes, and above all do it with a smile on your face!

After all, it is a game, and it is there to be enjoyed.

KP'S APPROACH TO CRICKET

KP

"I work hard at every single aspect of my game. It is so important to me that I practise with a purpose and with intensity, so that when I am out in the middle in a One-Day International or a Test match I give myself the best chance of success. By setting challenges in training with inspired and innovative drills, you can get the best out of yourself in every game situation."

Kevin Pietersen – England's premier batsman.

INTRODUCTION

WARM-UPS

Warm-ups are a vital part of every training session and game of cricket, but they don't just have to be boring stretches or jogging! Be inspired to get the most out of each and every warm-up, and keep them fun, challenging and exciting.

Why warm up?

i) Team-bonding: the warm-up is the first part of the session or game, and is a chance to get all of your players together, doing some skills or a game and interacting with each other. It not only signifies the start of your session, but if run properly can give everyone a chance to have a laugh and joke with each other.

ii) Related-skills: by trying some of the warm-ups in this section, you can get your players to start learning and practising skills and movement patterns that will be useful for them not only in cricket, but other sports as well. By using these movements and skills regularly each session they will become better at them and will ultimately start using them when needed during games.

iii) Physical factor: the warm-up gives you, the coach, a chance to start all of your players moving around in a reasonably controlled environment, and building up the intensity of movement so the players are ready for training, or a game situation. It gives players the opportunity to get blood flowing to the muscles that they are likely to be putting under pressure when they start getting competitive and moving at 100% intensity.

Think about these factors when preparing your warm-up:
- Start with slow dynamic movements like jogging, skipping and side-shuffling.
- Build up the intensity as the warm-up continues.
- Try to mimic movement patterns you are about to perform – e.g. if you're about to field, practise lunging into a pick-up, or bring in some arm movement if about to throw or bowl.
- Be inventive. Set up your warm-ups simply, but bring in new games and challenges to ignite the body and mind.

Over the next few pages are a number of controlled activities aimed at getting the best out of your players. So be inspired and enjoy your warm-ups.

PRO TIP

Justin Langer

"Warm-ups play a vital part in all of my cricket sessions. Proper preparation is vital in order to get my mind and body focused, and gives me the best chance of getting the most out of every training session or game."

Warm-ups: controlled and uncontrolled

Controlled
At the start of the session the coach should involve the players in a warm-up which starts with slow controlled movements, with the intensity and range of movement then increasing. If you go straight into a competitive warm-up game, players are likely to overstretch muscles that have not been warmed up. This doesn't have to be boring though, so try the games and drills explained over the following pages to get your players working through different ranges of motion whilst having fun at the same time. Be inspired…..

Uncontrolled
Once the coach is happy that the players have gone through a full range of drills and movement patterns in a controlled environment, it is good to play a warm-up game which will get the players moving faster, improving co-ordination and getting their heart rate up further. Hopefully by making these game-based drills, it will heighten the players' competitive edge, and get their minds into a sporting mode!

WARM-UPS

CONTROLLED
In the square

Set-up – four markers designating a space.

Action – players are asked to move around slowly in all different directions. Encourage forward, backward, and sideways movements. Also low skips, high skips, fast feet, high knees etc.

COACHING TIP

Warm-ups play a vital role for the modern-day cricketer. Not only do they provide a chance for players to get their bodies moving, and practise some skills, but they also provide an excellent opportunity for the team to bond and enjoy themselves on a match-day or training session.

VARIATIONS

The gearbox – four gears: walk, slow, medium, fast or 1, 2, 3, 4. Coach calls different gear and players respond accordingly. This can be done multi-directionally, or after designated call of forwards, backwards, or sideways.

Groups – at any point during any of the movement patterns, coach calls 'groups of 3' or 'groups of 5' for example. The last team to get together performs a forfeit (or players that do not make a group of the correct number).

Initials – coach calls out a letter, and any player whose first name or surname starts with that letter has to do a fast lap of the square, or touch a marker and then rejoin group.

'Montys' – at the coach's call of 'MONTY!', players must jump in the air and high-five each other until the coach shouts 'STOP', at which point players return to multi-directional movement. (This can be done with other cricketers with high-energy celebrations e.g. 'Brett Lee!', jump and punch air.)

Balls In – while players are moving around the square, introduce first one, then two, then three different balls (softer balls for younger players). Players must keep passing and catching balls, ensuring that both passer and receiver have made eye contact. If any ball hits the ground, the whole team performs a forfeit (e.g. 5 press-ups).

Be inventive with your variations, be Inspired.

Bases

Set-up – a number of bases are set up depending on the number of players. About three to five players per team. Bases are a group of 5-6 markers on the floor in a small circle only just big enough to fit 3-5 players in when standing. Make each base with a different set of coloured markers so that you have Blue base, Red base, Yellow base etc, and a corresponding blue team, red team and yellow team.

Action – bases are set 20-30m apart from all other bases, if you have 3, then in a large triangle. Players must stay within the area described by the position of the bases. Each team has one ball, and all players have to keep moving multi-directionally, passing the ball to each other. Call different movement patterns whilst they are doing this, such as backwards, sideways, low skips etc – NB PLAYERS MUST ALWAYS BE MOVING. When you call 'BASES', all players have to run to their base and huddle so that no part of any body is outside the base. The last team to do so performs a forfeit.

VARIATIONS

Opposites – change the call to 'OPPOSITION BASE', so teams are trying to fully inhabit an opposition area. The team who has the first player inside a base controls it, and last team to get all its players inside a base performs a forfeit.

Ball-swap – have each team passing and catching a different coloured ball. When the coach shouts 'CHANGE' the team has to swap the ball with another team before carrying on.

Roll and pick-ups – rather than passing and catching, teams have to roll the ball along the floor and pick it up while moving around, to practise cricket-based movements.

Cross-over grid

Set-up – sets of markers 5m apart, 6 different sets. Players in pairs starting at the first pair of markers (blue cones in diagram) with one ball between two.

Action – pair 1 stand opposite each other on the first set of markers (blue). They pass the ball between each other three times, before moving onto the next set of markers (red). However, in order to get to the next set of markers, they must cross over so they are now on the opposite side to the one they were on for the first set of passes. At this marker (red), they complete another three catches, and then cross over onto the next set of markers (yellow). In this way, they keep moving down the grid, crossing over each time, until they reach the far end, where they both run down the outside and back to the start. Each pair of players waits until the pair in front of them has completed their passes and made it to the next set of markers before they start.

VARIATIONS

The Chase – each pair is trying to catch up with the pair in front of them. This will put their catching and throwing skills under pressure, as they attempt to do it quickly.

Catch that! – each time the players have made it successfully through the circuit and back to the start, give them a different catching challenge. Left hand only, right hand only, above the head, right hand over left shoulder, left hand over right shoulder. Different catches means better hand-eye co-ordination.

Fielding skills – it doesn't just have to be catches. Bounce the ball once each time between the pairs, throw it on the half-volley each time, or roll it on the floor for a one-handed or two handed pick-up.

Movement patterns – when they are running back down the outside of the grid, call a different warm-up movement. 'High Knees', 'Low skips', 'Sideways facing the grid' etc. Remember this is a warm-up drill so they need to get warm!

WARM-UPS

Ladder circuit

Set-up – markers and ladders laid out (see picture).

Action – split players into two groups and form a queue behind each of the red markers. The first pair runs to central section (blue) keeping in time with their partner throughout, where they perform the movement pattern as called by the coach. They move from the end of the central section round the far yellow markers and back through the ladders where they perform footwork drill as called by coach, then back to their original queue. The second pair start when the previous pair reach the end of the blue markers.

Coach calls a variety of different movements through the central section to ensure that all muscle groups are warmed up.

VARIATIONS
Inspired – be inventive with what the players do through the blue section e.g. facing each other, performing high-hand slaps whilst side-stepping, or low-hand slaps. Give each pair a ball which they have to pass between them as many times as possible in central section.

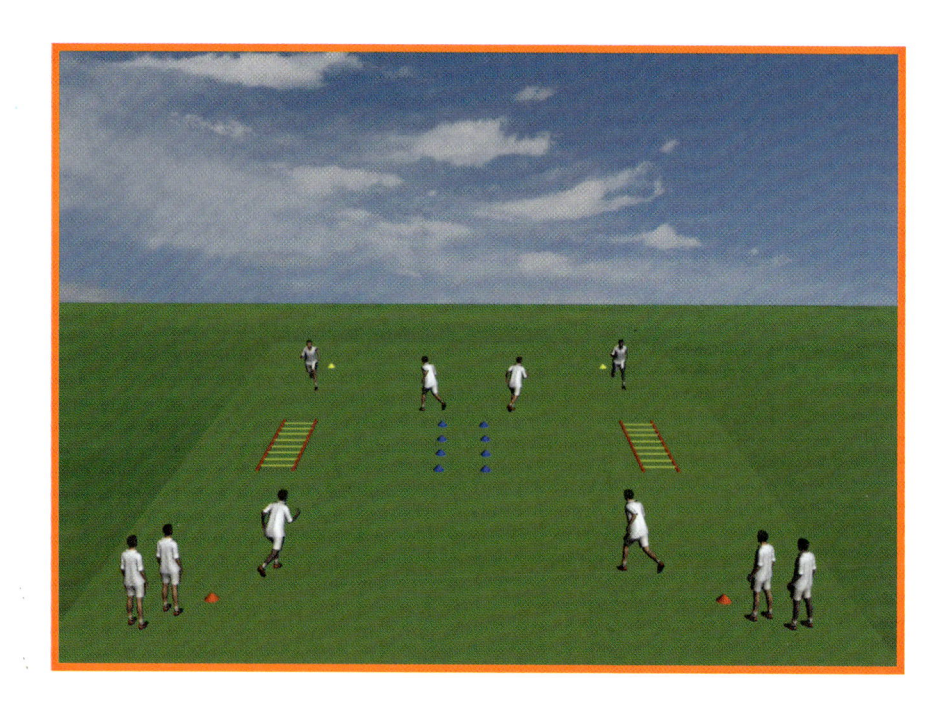

PRO TIP

Matt Maynard

"When training at any age, it's important to make the practice enjoyable and appropriate to the skills you will need in a game. Whether it is in warm-up games, fielding practice or batting and bowling in the nets, players need to challenge themselves to perform as they would do in a match situation. Providing a competitive and enjoyable environment every session will keep them coming back and improving all the time."

Military lap

Set-up – all you need is your players and a field for a new take on this old-school warm-up.

Action – players stay in a tight group and make their way slowly around the outfield awaiting further instructions from the coach.

Suggested Instructions:
Assign a different action to a different number, e.g. 1 = right hand down, 2 = left hand down, 3 = jump and catch, 4 = everyone flat on their backs. Call the numbers out to get players' minds and bodies working.

Perform pretend cricket-style actions, e.g. 1 = one-hand pick up and underarm throw, 2 = two-hand pick-up and overarm throw, 3 = bowling action, 4 = wicket-keeper's squat.

Groups – as player are jogging around, randomly call 'GROUPS OF 4' or some other number. The last players into a group perform a forfeit.

Simon Says – put a different spin on this practice by making it a game of Simon Says, or 'Brunchy Says' (input your own name to the game's title!). Try to catch your players out by telling them that they must only perform the action if 'Brunchy Says'. Any player that performs the action if you don't say your name prior to the action performs a forfeit.

WARM-UPS

American Football drill

Set-up – organise your players into lines of three to four across, with as many lines deep as you have players, eg with nine players have three lines of three players. The coach stands at the front of the players facing them all.

Action – all of the players must start gently jogging on the spot. The coach tells the players four different hand signals, which result in four different actions. If the coach points his hand out to the side, all players lunge towards that direction and pretend to pick up a ball. This happens to the left and to the right. If the coach points up, all players have to jump in the air and land in the coil position like a fast bowler. If the coach points down, all players have to go down into full wicket-keeping crouch then straight back up to their original position. Any player who does the wrong action performs a forfeit.

VARIATIONS:

Batting specific – players all face the coach and jog on the spot but in their batting stance pretending to have bat in hands. The coach's different hand signals result in different pretend shots being played by the players. E.g. coach points left, players play a cut shot, coach points right, players play a leg glance, coach points down, players play a straight drive, coach points up players play a pull shot.

Speed drills – once the players are a bit warmer, the coach can make them move more quickly. Progress onto following instructions: Players start in 'ready' position as if they are a fielder. Coach points arm out to side and players all turn and run 5m in the direction of the arm. Coach points down, players squat down like a wicket-keeper then jump as high as they can. Coach points up and players have to half turn and run back 5m as if taking catch overhead.

Matchplay – you can turn this drill into a knock-out competition if you like. Set up your four instructions, and then perform them – any player to go the wrong way or do the wrong action is out. Players who hesitate significantly are also out. Get down to a final and a winner.

Opposites – to make it even harder for older or more competent players, they have to go the opposite way to that which you point, eg right = left, up = down.

COACHING TIP

Make sure players have enough room between them so that if they run towards each other they do not clash and injure themselves!

WARM-UPS

Dynamic shuttles

Set-up – two lines of markers about 20m apart, wide enough for all players to fit next to each other.

Action – classic warm-up and way to ensure all players have gone through a range of movement patterns prior to any more vigorous drills. Players move forward as a group performing the same movement, then return as a group once they have reached far set of markers. Start with simple slow jogging, and increase movements by kicking bums, high knees, side-shuffles, low skips, high skips, fast feet, lunges, etc.

VARIATIONS

Cricket-specific – introduce cricket-style movement patterns to be practised without ball e.g. one-handed pick-up and flick, two-handed pick-up and throw, bowling action, pull-shot, hit over top.

The wave – as players are jogging backwards and forwards, the player nearest the coach responds to the first new movement (e.g. high knees), all other players just jog as normal. When players turn for the next shuttle, coach calls new movement (e.g. sideways facing me), which the player nearest him now performs. The second player performs the first movement (high knees) and all others jog. On third turn coach calls new movement (e.g. low skip) which first player performs. Now third player performs high knees, second player performs sideways, others jog. In this way all of the movement patterns travel down the line in a wave. Any mistakes result in a forfeit.

Player calls – put the emphasis back on the players. Work your way down the line with each player calling a new movement pattern. Any repeats result in a forfeit. Encourage imitation of sporting stars to elicit different movements e.g 'ROONEY' call results in players pretending to kick a football, or 'SHAQUILLE O'NEAL' call players jump and slam-dunk a pretend basketball.

COACHING TIP
Remember to start slowly and build up!

UNCONTROLLED
The chase

Set-up – designate an area, size depending upon the number of players. All players have a bib hanging out of the back of their shorts/trousers.

Action – designate one or two players as chasers (depending on number of players, if more than 8 suggest 2). They then have to chase the other players around inside the playing area. If a chaser pulls the bib out of another player's shorts, that player joins the chasers, until there is only one player left. The larger the area, the harder it will be for the chasers.

WARM-UPS

Keep ball

Set-up – mark out a playing area, whatever shape and size you like, but enough for all of your players to move around in. Split players into two teams with bibs.

Action – there is one ball in the playing area. A player with the ball in their hand cannot move. The aim of the game is for their team to successfully complete 10 catches in a row, without the ball being intercepted or hitting the floor. If the ball hits the floor, regardless of who it touched last, it is a turnover of possession. Team scores a point by completing 10 passes, coach decides how many points wins the game depending upon time available. If player has ball in possession and steps out of playing area then possession turns over.

VARIATIONS

Harder catch – use the same rules as above but make it one-hand catching only, or 'wrong'-hand catching only.

No pass-backs – make the rule that players CAN'T pass back to the person that passed to them.

Roll-ball – as above but the ball has to be rolled along floor to a team member and cleanly picked up to complete a pass.

WARM-UPS

Cricket-football

Set-up – use markers to designate a scoring area, perhaps a small 2m x 2m square, one at either end of a pitch. Players are split into two teams with bibs. Pitch size depends upon number of players per team.

Action – players score a goal by standing in the scoring area and catching the ball from one of their team-mates. Opposition players are not allowed in the scoring area they are defending. Players cannot move if they have the ball in their hands, but have to advance up the pitch towards the scoring area by throwing the ball to each other, and moving whilst not in possession of the ball. If the ball hits the floor, or the player moves whilst the ball is in possession then it is a turnover. If a defender steps in the opposition's scoring area, it is a penalty. To score a penalty, one teammate must stand in their own scoring area, and throw overarm to a teammate standing in the opposition scoring area, without that teammate moving out of the area.

VARIATIONS

Harder catch – perform same game but one-handed catching only.

Cricket-specific – perform same game but rolling ball along floor instead of throwing.

Bouncy – perform same game but ball has to bounce once between each pass.

Score Zone – try using different shapes and sizes of scoring area to make the game different each session.

Vortex/frisbee

Set-up – create either a scoring box (3m x 3m) with markers, or an 'End Zone' a bit like a rugby try-zone which spans the end of the pitch (see example in diagram). Players split into two teams with bibs.

Action – players score by completing a pass to a player standing in the scoring zone. Players CAN move with the 'frisbee' in their hands, but if they are tagged by a member of the opposition, then possession changes hands. A team has to complete six passes before they can score a goal, and you can't pass back to the player who passed to you.

COACHING TIP

Using a Vortex or a frisbee challenges the players to catch an object which moves in a different way to a normal ball. This will improve their hand-eye co-ordination and help them to watch the 'ball' in flight more carefully.

WARM-UPS

Four-goal 'fandango'!

Set-up – four scoring areas are set up, with pairs of coloured markers approximately 1.5m apart (see diagram). Players are split into two teams with bibs.

Action – players cannot move when the ball is in their hand. They must pass by throwing the ball to each other. A point can be scored – after completing a minimum of five passes – by rolling the ball along the floor through ANY of the scoring areas, as long as a team-mate picks up the ball cleanly once it has passed through the scoring area. Players can move ANYWHERE. Once a team has scored they swap possession over. Players dropping the ball or fumbling results in possession turn-over and resetting of the pass-count.

VARIATIONS

Catch only – players have to pass the ball to each other under head height but on the full. Any time the ball hits the floor possession turns over. You score by under-arming the ball through a goal and it being caught on the other side.

Roll only – as above but all passes must roll along the floor to encourage fielding skills. Again, the ball must be cleanly fielded after passing through a goal to count.

No returns – introduce the rule that players can't return the ball to the player that passed to them

One-hand – players are only allowed to use one hand. This can work when either catching, or rolling the ball on the floor.

Bouncy-Bouncy – if the surface allows, players must bounce the ball once, but only once, as they pass to each other, and the ball must also bounce once (and only once) as they score.

COACHING TIP

If any players are seen goal-hanging, or standing still, send them for a lap of the four goals (or to a press-up 'sin-bin'). This is a warm-up remember so they need to be getting warm!

FIELDING – AGILITY

Agility drills

Here are some simple to set up agility drills that are not only fun and challenging for players of all ages, but will also test their skills of moving quickly and in a coordinated manner.

These drills will specifically test the player's ability to turn and make short, sharp movements – the sort of movements that can make all of the difference between stopping the ball or missing it; taking the catch or it being just out of reach; turning effectively when running between the wickets to gain that extra few centimetres.

All of these benefits from a few fun drills!

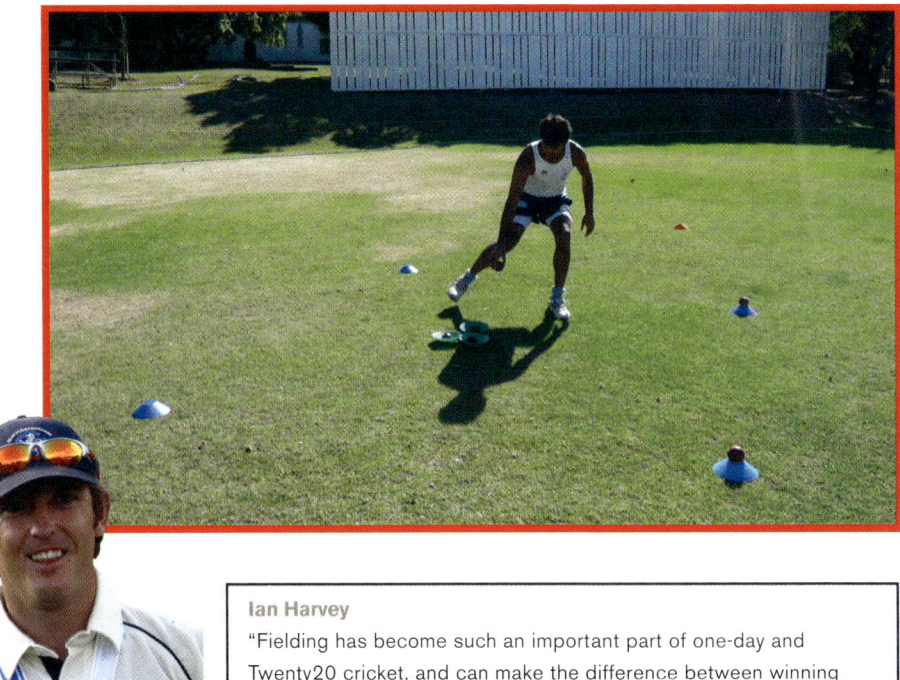

PRO TIP

Ian Harvey
"Fielding has become such an important part of one-day and Twenty20 cricket, and can make the difference between winning and losing a game! I always make sure that I'm practising my skills at catching, throwing at stumps and making diving stops. This gives me the best chance of fielding well in a match situation……..plus it's great fun if you can make the drills competitive and challenging!"

Fielding star

Set-up – set out eight markers to signify the points of a star, with either a bucket/container or some upturned cones in the middle of the star. Place a ball on each of the outer eight markers.

Action – the player starts in the middle of the star, and their job is to retrieve each ball from each point marker in turn, placing it safely into the container in the middle. They must ensure that the ball is stationary in the middle before heading out for the next retrieval. Once all the balls are safely in the middle, the next player must put them all back out again, ensuring they are stationary on the marker before returning for the next pick-up. You can set up as many stars as you like, so that no more than four players are working in each star.

VARIATIONS

Stopwatch – once they have practicsed, try timing each player to make it competitive. Can they beat each other and their best time?

Race – start two players on opposite sides of the star, with only half of the balls laid out on the markers. Player 1 has to retrieve all of the balls into the middle, whilst player 2 is trying to put all of the balls out. Make sure they are going round in the same direction to avoid any collisions! Do this until one player makes a mistake, or for a set time period.

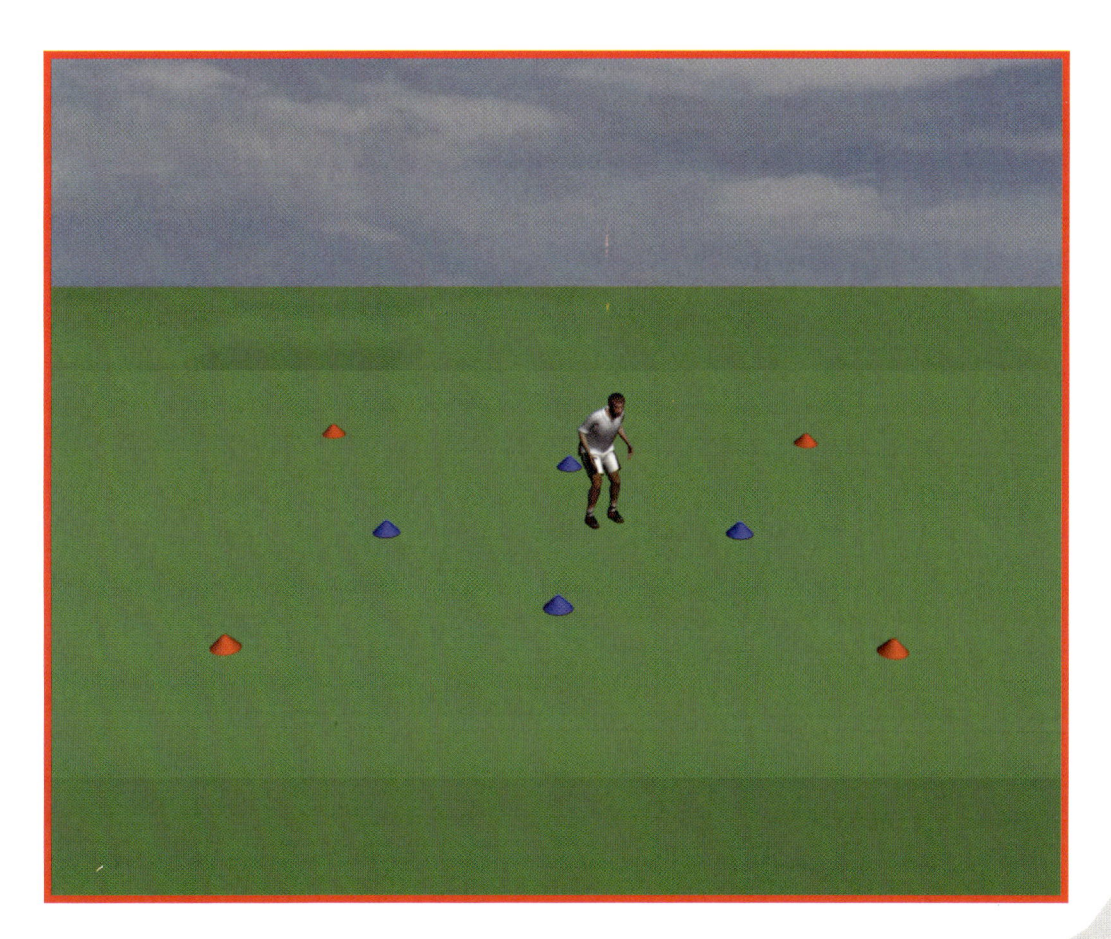

Catch-2

Set-up – players are put into groups of three. Each trio has two players with a ball (feeders), and one player without a ball (catcher). The catcher starts between two markers with feeders facing them in line with the markers (see diagram).

Action – the catcher assumes a ready position, and feeder 1 (left) throws a short underarm catch, which makes the catcher move before catching the ball. Once they have caught it, they return the ball. As soon as they have returned the ball, feeder number 2 (right) provides a catch which makes the catcher move the other way. This continues until the catcher has taken ten in a row.
If the catcher has to dive to make the catch, make sure the feeder lets them back onto their feet before releasing the next catch. Once the catcher has completed ten catches, each player moves round one position clockwise.

COACHING TIP

Timing is everything in this drill. The feeders have a VERY important job, to make sure the catcher has to move, but not make the catches out of reach. If you can get the timing right – it's a great drill for fast feet and changing direction.

The pod

Set-up – each pod consists of four different coloured markers, in a 2m x 2m diamond shape. The working player starts in the middle of the pod, facing one of the markers (see diagram). Players are in twos or threes at each pod.

Action – one of the non-working players is the 'caller'. They call out a colour, and the working player has to move as quickly as possible to get their feet either side of the marker of that colour, and then return to the middle of the pod. As soon as they get back to the middle, the next colour is called. This is supposed to be a fast moving game, with the players reacting to a verbal cue. The player continues to call different colours until the working player either makes a mistake, or gets ten right in a row. Then the next player jumps into the pod, ready for action.

VARIATIONS

NESW – instead of a colour, name the markers North, East, South and West. Now call a direction each time. This will test the players' brains as well as their bodies!

Numbers – try giving each marker a number 1-4 instead of a colour. Different players will find numbers, colours, directions easier and harder.

Mix-it! – if the players are getting really good at each of the above, start mixing up the colours, numbers and directions all into the one go. 'Red', 'North', '3', 'Blue' etc. This can get really fun!

COACHING TIP

Timing of the call is important again, give the player enough time to get back to the middle of the pod, but not too much time to settle before they have to make their next move. This is an agility drill so changes of direction are good!

Ladder work 1

If you have an agility ladder or two in your kit-bag they can be turned into cricket-based drills quite easily.

Set-up – lay out the ladder on the floor so that there is some room either end. Set out some markers either end of the ladder (see diagram). You will also need to position feeders at various stages.

COACHING TIP

If you don't have a ladder and you are working indoors, you can just draw a ladder on the floor with chalk! It's just a way of making the players think about their movements…..

FIELDING – AGILITY

Action – players are going to work laterally along the ladder in both directions.

1. The first drill is for them to just take it in turns going along the ladder sideways – quickly stepping into each gap with both feet whilst facing forward, and getting used to the lateral movement.

2. Next time through have a feeder half way along the ladder, with a ball. As the player passes they have to take a catch and return it to the feeder whilst still moving.

3. Now have two or three feeders along the ladder, so the player has to catch and move all the way down.

4. Now set up two differently coloured markers at each end of the ladder (see diagram), and a feeder waiting with a ball in hand. As the player comes off the end of the ladder laterally, the feeder calls a colour, and the player has to run to that marker before making a catch.

Ladder work 2

Set-up – have the ladder placed on the ground with plenty of space off the end of it, as the players are to run through facing forwards. You need different markers available to adapt the drill after players have come through the ladder (see diagram).

COACHING TIP

The 'set' position is the position players should get into just before the batsman plays a shot whenever they are fielding. It's a ready position, with knees slightly bent, weight on the balls of their feet and hands out in front of their body. Imagine a goalkeeper in football getting ready to make a save...

FIELDING – AGILITY

Action – this drill encourages the players to come through the ladder with coordinated footwork, (e.g. two feet in each gap), but also to practise their 'set' position off the end of the ladder.

1) Have a feeder off the end of the ladder with a ball, and once the player has come through the ladder, and got into their 'set' position, the feeder provides a catch. This can start straight at the player, then progress to harder and harder catches to either side.

2) Have three different coloured markers set out 5m away from the end of the ladder on different angles. When the player comes through and gets set, call a colour, and they have to move quickly to that marker before taking a catch.

3) As with number 2), but this time roll the ball on the floor so the player has to move and make a stop. Put the players under the maximum pressure they can handle, so they get used to moving fast and making important stops in the field.

Be inspired with this type of training – there are limitless ways in which you can adapt these simple drills to get agile and coordinated movement which is relevant to cricket.

FIELDING – THROWING-BASED

Introduction

Fielding is such an important part of modern-day cricket that it's imperative that players of all ages are given the opportunity for some quality practice. And the best way to get everyone practising is to make your drills fun and innovative, letting the players learn through practice.

This section is split into two parts – throwing-based fielding drills, and catching-based drills, although some of the drills contain elements of both.

Major coaching point – THROWING

In all of the throwing-based drills, try to encourage the players to line their feet up at their target as much as possible. They need to plant their feet on the ground, and draw an imaginary line from big toe to big toe, and if this line were to continue on from their front leg, it should point towards the target they are aiming for (see diagram).

COACHING TIP

A simple way to get players to tell if their bodyweight is going towards their target is to get them to follow-through towards the stumps.

Direct hits

Set-up – three sets of stumps are set out 1m apart from each other. One set has all three stumps, one set has just two stumps, and one set has only one stump. Four markers are set out to signify a large rectangle with the stumps in the middle.

Action – players are split into two teams. First team go to the far corner and take it in turns to pick-up and throw at the stumps. The other team are backing up. They start in the opposite corner and move into position as the thrower is picking up the ball.

1-2-3 – as the player picks the ball up, they have the choice of which set of stumps to aim at. If they hit the set of 3, they get 1 point. If they hit the 2, they get 2 points, and if they hit the 1 stump, they get 3 points. Each player in the team has a throw and points are added up. Then the second team attempts to beat this.

Move round to have a go from each of the corners and add up all the points for a team championship.

Dynamic run saving

Set-up – set of stumps in the middle with keeper and/or coach next to them, then six markers laid out to signify six different starting points for fielders, at differing distances (see diagram).

Activity – players are split in two, and line up behind each of the green markers. Keeper or coach rolls ball out towards first player (right green marker) who attacks it, and returns, before swapping to the back of the opposite queue of players (left green marker). Keeper then rolls out to the player at the left green marker, who returns and goes to opposite queue. Continue this until everyone has had two goes from each green marker, then both queues move back to the next set of markers, a bit further away (white). Repeat the above although this time players should throw in overarm before swapping queues.

Set the markers so that the closest pair are having to quickly attack the ball from a one-saving position, and the next set so that they are having to throw overarm, from a position similar to that in the ring. Try hitting high catches to the players at the farthest set of markers.

FIELDING – THROWING-BASED

VARIATIONS

Action – slow to fast. Start off slowly, encouraging players to make sure they pick the ball up cleanly before throwing, but as they go through the round encourage them to attack the ball as much as they can whilst still in control.

Angles – if the players are doing well with the ball coming straight at them, feed the ball a few metres inside the line of the marker, so they have to move their feet around to get their body back in line with the ball. Remember the ball doesn't always come straight at you in a game! This can be done at all different distances.

Challenge 1 – give each player a mark out of 2 for every piece of fielding, 1 mark for clean pick-up, and 1 mark for good throw. Set them a target score at one distance which they have to beat individually before they can move onto the next set of markers.

Challenge 2 – try the above challenge, but split the players into two teams and keep a total for each side, so that the players start to feel the pressure of a game situation!

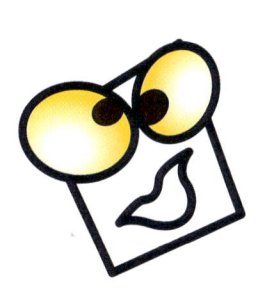

COACHING TIP

Try getting your players to think about the skill in two phases – 'the pick-up' & 'the throw'. Remind them that they can't move onto phase two before they've completed phase one!

Four stations, four jobs

Set up – you need five markers and a set of stumps. Set them up (see diagram) with a central line of four markers, one of which is the stumps. The other two markers are about 15m away from the set of stumps.

Activity – the coach/keeper starts on the marker nearest the stumps (red). One player is on marker number 2 (white) and one player is on marker 4 (yellow), both with a ball in hand. The rest of the players are split in half with one queue of players behind each of the remaining markers, green and blue. Each of the markers represents a different skill that needs to be performed, and these are going on at the same time, resulting in everyone being involved in a great fun fielding drill (sounds complicated but is easy once you get going).

Station 1 – coach/keeper (red) rolls ball out, player attacks from blue marker, picks up and throws at the stumps.

Station 2 – after throwing at the stumps, player from blue runs on to white marker to receive an underarm flick fed by player. Players swap and player previously on station 2 (white) runs onto back of queue at station 3 (green).

Station 3 – player moves from green into an appropriate position to back up the throw at stumps from station 1, then throws back to the keeper (red) before moving onto station 4 (yellow).

Station 4 – player on station 4 (yellow) feeds an underarm catch to oncoming player. Players swap, player from station 4 (yellow) runs to back of queue at station 1 (blue).

NB Once started this drill continues in a circle so that everyone is moving all of the time!

FIELDING – THROWING-BASED

VARIATIONS

2 and 4 – you can be a bit inventive on stations 2 and 4, depending on what you want your players to practise; one-handed pick-up, two-handed pick-up, wrong-handed pick-up, low catch, head-high catch, high catch, one-handed catch are just a few of the options.

Different balls – try having different balls on stations 2 and 4, maybe a golf ball, or a tennis ball, or even a rugby ball! It will give a different challenge for the players to catch the different balls which will help general hand-eye co-ordination.

COACHING TIP

Encourage the players to be the best they can at EVERY station – there are lots of skills being challenged in this drill.

The Grid

Set-up – two stumps about 10m apart (each with keeper or coach with baseball mitt on them), and a marker opposite each stump about 10m away, creating a 10m x 10m square (see diagram).

Activity – this is a great pick-up and throw drill, which can be used to practise throws of all different angles. Players are split into two groups, lined up behind the marker opposite a keeper or mitt-man. Keeper rolls the ball straight out to the player, who picks it up and throws it back before heading to the back of the queue (see picture 1).

FIELDING – THROWING-BASED

VARIATIONS

Keeper 1 now rolls ball out to the inside of the player in queue 1 (red marker), who returns it to the opposite catcher (keeper 2), and then joins the back of the opposite queue (blue maker). This ball is still 'live', as it is then rolled out by keeper 2 to the inside of his queue (blue marker), and returned to keeper number 1 (see picture 2).

Keeper 1 now rolls the ball to the outside of queue 1 (red), so the player has to pick up, spin and throw to opposite keeper (2). This is repeated at the other side.

COACHING TIP

This is a great drill for practising getting your feet in line towards your target, as the ball will be coming on a number of different angles. Get players to try different techniques in order to get into position most efficiently.

FIELDING – THROWING-BASED

Quickfire stump hitting

Set-up – put five single stumps in the ground, with five blue markers opposite about 10m away. Place a ball on each blue marker. Have five different coloured markers (yellow) set out in line with the blue ones, also about 10m away from the stumps (see diagram).

Action – the working player starts at the red marker, runs out to the first ball (on blue), and throws at the stump, before running back around stump number 1, and repeating the above, until there have been throws at each of the five stumps. Each stump has another player backing up behind it, starting from the white cone. They move along the line backing up each of the throws. Once the first pair has finished, the next pair can start. Add up the scores and make it competitive!

VARIATIONS

Time challenge – to put the players under more pressure, time how long it takes for them to complete the five stump challenge. To make it interesting, you could take three seconds off their total time for each hit.

Roll-outs – to make it more realistic and harder, the player runs out to the marker, and the coach rolls a ball out to them for a pick up and throw. This is done at each of the five stations.

Fielding races 1

Set-up – with good planning, you can set up for all three of the different races suggested below. You'll need two sets of stumps and seven markers. See the diagram for set-up. One of the teams will need to have bats in their hands (blue team in diagrams).

Action – players are split into two teams. Each player will race individually against an opponent, with the batsmen trying to complete a run whilst the fielders are trying to run them out.

Race 1 – run one vs underarm flick.
This is a straight race. The batting team line up behind their starting marker (yellow), and can only start running when the ball is released to the fielding team. The batting team has to ground their bat past the stumps before the fielder completes a pick-up and underarm flick having started at the red marker. Each player has a turn before the teams swap over.

Fielding races 2

Race 2 – run two vs pick up and over-arm throw.

Now the batting team start at their stumps, and have to try to run a two touching down past the yellow marker before the opposition can run them out. The fielding team start between the blue markers on the right. Both players set off when the coach releases the ball, and the fielding player must run across to the ball and return it to the stumps, before the batter can run a two.

COACHING TIP

For the coach/feeder, this is a potentially tricky feed, as the distance has to be right to make it a good race. In general, make it so that if the fielder does everything right (i.e. attacks, picks up & good throw) then they should get the run out by a metre or so.

FIELDING – THROWING-BASED

Fielding races 3

Race 3 – finally, the batting team have to try to run a three (starting at the yellow marker), before their opposite number has sprinted out to the far WHITE cone, picked a ball up from on top of the cone and thrown it back to the coach.

Variation – the coach can roll out a ball for the retrieval game, but it is best to have a target distance in mind in order to keep the race a fair one!

COACHING TIP

You might have to adjust the distance that the white cone is away from the coach, so that it is a good race between the fielding team and the batting team!

FIELDING – CATCHING-BASED

Introduction

As everyone has heard many times, 'catches win matches', and the reason this saying has been around for so long is because it is the truth! No matter what level you are playing at, whether it's for your local under 11s, or for England in the Ashes, every single catch is vital to the success of your team. Because they are so important, it is essential that players have practised the skills of catching as hard as any other skill in the game. The drills in this section aim to provide a variety of different types of catching, so that whatever height, speed or trajectory the ball comes in a game, each player has the ability to deal with it successfully.

COACHING TIP

To give yourself the best chance of catching the ball, spread your hands wide as the ball is on its way. This gives a bigger surface area for the ball to hit. Close the hands around the ball as it makes contact with your palms.

COACHING TIP

There are many aspects which contribute to catching a ball, but one thing that is incredibly important is to **WATCH THE BALL!** It's amazing how many players take their eyes off the ball at some point during its flight before it's firmly lodged in their hands. Keep your eyes on the ball, and to do this you have to get your head in a good position! Go on give it a go!

The Snake

Set-up – all you need for this is a few balls (it doesn't really matter if they are cricket balls, tennis balls, Kwik Cricket balls etc), and all of your players. Split the players into two groups, and get them into two lines, facing each other. Each player should be about 2m away from the player next to them, and the lines should be 3m apart (see diagram).

Action – the ball starts at one end of the line, and the player underarms it across to the first person in the line opposite them, and then runs down the outside of his line to join the far end. The player opposite catches the ball, then passes it to the next person in the opposite line, before running down the outside and joining the far end of the same line. The ball keeps moving down the line, crossing over each time. This forms a never-ending 'snake' as the players from the near end move to the far end so that there's always someone to catch the ball.

FIELDING – CATCHING-BASED

VARIATIONS

Set the team a target distance to reach with their 'snake', without anyone dropping the ball.

2-3-4 – if the team is managing to move the snake well, it's time to make it harder! After the first ball gets started, instead of the players moving down the outside straight away, they have to wait for the second ball to be introduced. This follows the other one down the snake. Tell the players how many balls they have to wait for until they can move.

One-hand – try doing the same but with only one hand catching. How about using two different coloured balls, RED ones caught in the right hand only, YELLOW ones caught in the left hand.

Hand-eye coordination

Set-up – get the players in pairs, and have a number of different balls available e.g. different colours, weights, textures and sizes.

Action – start with simple catching between pairs. Then move to one hand only, working both left and right hands. Now try getting them to catch two balls at the same time, crossing them over in the middle. Let them have a go at catching two balls at the same time – one in each hand. Can they both catch two balls at the same time, with both pairs crossing in between them? Throw two different coloured balls and call a colour as you throw – the player only catches the coloured ball that is called.

FIELDING – CATCHING-BASED

VARIATIONS

Compete – you can make this competitive by getting a hard drill, such as both players catching two balls at the same time, and making each pair perform in front of the group with everyone counting the number of complete catches. Remember each group's score for winners and losers.

Inspired – being inspired and inventive is the key with these drills. Anything that challenges the coordination and catching skills of your players will be of benefit to them. Give them a challenge to work out some new drills themselves.

COACHING TIP

Different groups will progress at different speeds, so observe that they are doing well at a skill before making it harder for them.

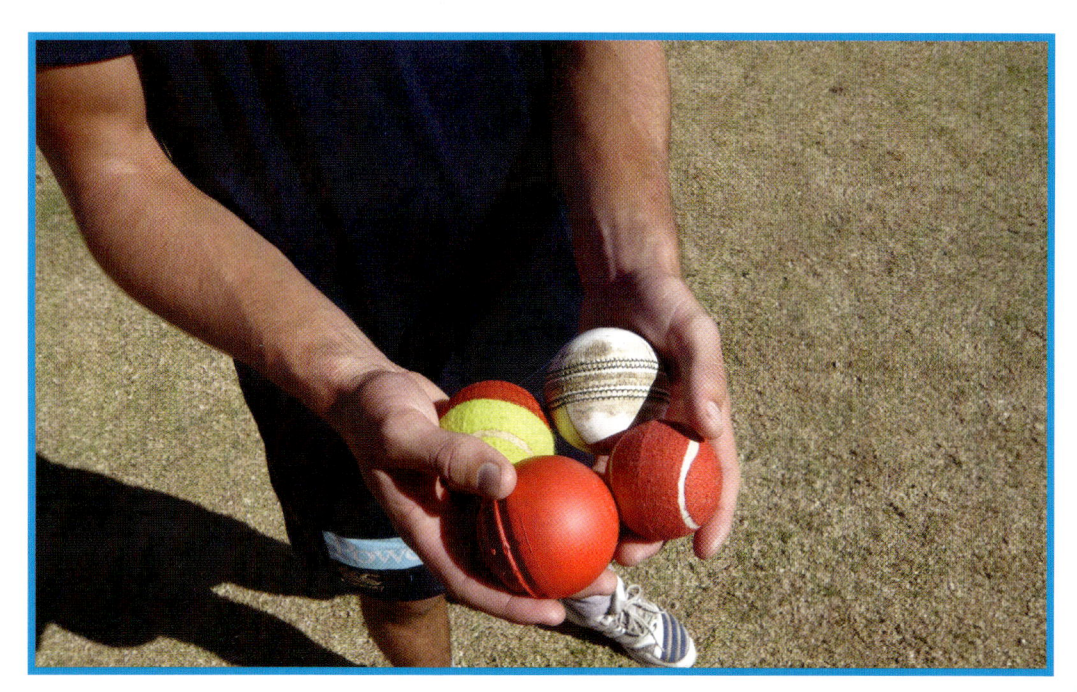

Quadrangle quick hands

Set-up – players get into groups of four, with one ball. They stand about 3m apart from each other in a square.

Action – the ball can travel two different ways around the square, either clockwise or anti-clockwise. If the ball is travelling clockwise, a right-handed player puts weight into their left-foot towards their target, and throws underarm. A left-handed player steps towards their target with their left foot and throws out of the back of the hand to the next player. Once started, the ball should move around the square as quickly as possible, with accurate throws and concentration on catching! The coach shouts 'Change', and whichever player has the ball then must release it in the opposite direction, with right-handers throwing out the back of the hand, and left-handers throwing out of the front of the hand.

VARIATION

For the advanced group if they are fizzing the ball around the quadrangle quickly, and changing direction well, then you could introduce two balls. Starting on opposite sides of the square this will really test the speed and reactions of the players (use a softer ball for this one).

Baseball racing game

Set-up – you need a set of stumps, and five markers set out as in the diagram. The marker in the middle has a ball placed upon it. This game is best played with five players on each team, however with a minimum of six players you can race each player individually.

Action – players are split into two teams, a fielding team and a running team. Only one of the running team takes part in each race. The running player and fielding player 1 both start at the stumps. When the coach shouts 'GO', it is the goal for the running player to run all the way round the outside of the markers and back past the stumps. In order for the fielding team to get a run-out, fielder 1 (at stumps) runs out and picks up the ball for the green marker, throwing it to fielder 2 (blue marker). Fielder 2 throws it across to fielder 3 (white marker), 3 throws to 4 (red marker), 4 throws to 5 (yellow marker), and then 5 throws it back to fielder 1, who should have run back to the stumps to effect a run-out. If the stumps are broken before the running player passes the stumps, it's a run-out! Each player has a go being the runner, with a different fielding position for the fielders each time.

VARIATION
Change-up – if players are good at performing the original method, then try changing the order in which the fielding team have to throw the ball to keep them thinking!

COACHING TIP
Make it competitive, count up the run-outs, and then swap teams to see which side can win.

American football overhead catching

Set-up – this drill has to be played outside, as you need a bit of space, and either a coach or players with a reasonable throwing arm! (as well as a few cricket balls….)

Action – the general idea here is to get players catching the ball whilst they are on the run. The coach/feeder starts with the ball in their hand. The player starts to run from the blue marker on an angle away from the coach, not looking at them. At any given point (chosen by the player) they change their angle of running and look back whilst still going on an angle away from the coach. The coach then throws the ball over their head as if they are a quarterback in American Football, so that the player has to run onto it and catch it. The ball returns and then the next player starts running.

VARIATION

Cut-back – another variation to change the type of catch taken, is for the player to cut back straight across in front of the coach, rather than continue away from them. If the coach sees that this is the movement, they throw a flat head high catch to the player.

Left-right – players can run away from the coach at any angle, to the left or the right. Encourage the players to try different angles and changes of direction to increase their learning.

FIELDING – CATCHING-BASED

Weakest link catching

Set-up – all you need for this one is two markers, a few balls and either a bat or racquet.

Action – get your players to line up in a queue in front of you, about 5-10m away. The front player walks towards you and just as you are about to strike the ball at them, they get into their 'set' position. You hit the ball, they catch it and move to the back of the queue. Then it's the next players turn. Have a target number of catches to be taken without dropping any – otherwise its back to 0! Give them a lifeline, though. If the target is 20, they can 'bank' at 12, which means that any drop after 12 only comes back to that number, but remember they must call 'Bank' otherwise it doesn't count!

VARIATION

Group specific – decide on the number of catches in total, and the 'bank' target depending on the age and skill level of the group. Also you could set a high target e.g 50, with more than one 'bank', e.g. 15 and 30.

Challenge – if any players are finding it easy in the group, give them a special challenge to catch their turn left hand only, or right hand only.

Compete – if you have a larger group, split them into several lines with a feeder at the front of each. See which team can get to their target first.

COACHING TIP

This is a really simple drill which puts the players under a bit of pressure, just like they would experience in a game! They don't want to be the Weakest Link!

FIELDING – CATCHING-BASED

Pairs high catching

Set-up – you need a bat and a ball. Or a tennis racquet and tennis ball depending on age/skill level of players (and hitting skills of the coach!).

Action – coach starts next to the stumps, and keeper is on the stumps ready to take return throw. Player starts next to the stumps as well. Coach hits the ball high in the air, and only when the ball is struck can the player turn and run from their starting position to try to get under the high catch. Once they've made the catch, they throw the ball back over the stumps.

COACHING TIP

You can make this competitive by counting up how many catches each player takes in a set number of goes, or get progressively harder and players get eliminated if they drop one.

VARIATIONS

Pairs – (see diagram) with a slightly larger group of players, send them out in pairs. Both have to start at the same time, one calls the catch and when they've taken it, pass it to their partner to throw back to keeper. Encourage thrower to be within 2m of the catcher when the catch is taken.

Blind catch – set up with both players facing away from the way they are going to run. They are only allowed to turn and look for the ball once they've heard the ball on the bat! One catches, and one throws back.

Fitness catching – not for the faint-hearted. Set a challenge of a number of catches, e.g. eight per pair. The first player catches the first half and passes to their partner to throw back to the keeper, and vice-versa for the second half. The coach tries to time it so that the players have to run and catch each one, and the partner has to be within 2m of each catch. It's harder than it sounds!

Goaltending

Set-up – simply two markers, placed on the ground to signify the 'goalposts' (see diagram). These can be closer or further apart depending on the age and skill level of the players.

Action – the aim of this drill is for the player to catch everything that comes at him/her, within the goalposts. Either the coach or one of the players has a bat (or tennis racquet) and hits the ball at catchable height somewhere between the goalposts. Players can either take it in turns to get 'set' and take a catch, then move out of the way for the next player in the group, or take a defined number of catches in a row.

COACHING TIP

Every now and again rather than hitting the ball at the goal, send a high catch up into the sky, this will keep the players on their toes!

FIELDING – CATCHING-BASED

VARIATIONS

Mix-ups – try using a cricket bat and a tennis racquet, tennis balls, Kwik-cricket balls, bowling machine balls, golf balls to test the players' ability to catch absolutely anything.

Sweeps – to make this even more game-realistic, you can set up the feeder on one knee ready to sweep the ball at the goal. Get one of the other players to feed the ball on the full, which will get the players into the habit of timing their 'set' position to the point at which the ball is struck.

Movement – in order to get the players catching on the move, call either 'left' or 'right' before you hit the catch. The player has to touch the corresponding marker, then make it back to the middle to take the catch.

Relay catching

Set-up – split your players into teams of three (in diagram there are yellow bib team, blue bib team, and white shirt team). Each team has a lane, signified by a near end-zone (red and yellow markers), and a far end-zone (blue and white markers). There's about 15-20m between the yellow and blue markers.

Action – this practice is a way of putting simple catching drills under pressure, and making it competitive in your team. Two players start at the nearest catching zone (red and yellow) with a ball, and the third player waits at the far catching zone (on white marker). Players trade five catches between each other at the red and yellow markers, before player at the red marker runs through to the blue marker. Five more catches are made between the blue and white markers, and player at white marker then through to the yellow marker (player previously on yellow has moved to red). This continues, with five catches at each of the end-zones until players are back in their starting positions. It's a race, so first team back wins!

FIELDING – CATCHING-BASED

VARIATION

Numbers/Styles – this is a really flexible drill which can be changed in many ways during one session. Change the number of catches needed at each end, or make the players take one handed catches.

Two balls – test the hand-eye skills even more by having a ball in each player's hand.

At the end zone the players have to perform cross-over catches before being able to run back.

Keep score – you can repeat this as many times as you like with different challenges each time. Try giving points for 1st and 2nd place, and add them up over the session.

COACHING TIP

This is a already a drill with a bit of fitness involved – but you can make it even more challenging by adding a certain number of press-ups, sit-ups or star-jumps in before they can start catching!

NET PRACTICE – INTRODUCTION

Nets – interesting, challenging, inspired....

The standard net session involves a series of batsmen going in to have a hit for 5-10mins at a time, until the coach shouts 'LAST THREE, YOUR TARGET IS 10!', or something of that nature.

Be INSPIRED! This age-old method of practising may be useful for your first net of pre-season, but you can get so much more out of each and every session with a bit of preparation.

Let's challenge the batsmen, challenge the bowlers, keep scores, have aims and targets, and try to learn something every single session either about yourself or about the game. Every time you bat in the middle you have to overcome the opposition, and take on a challenge, so why not train for success? Players learn more about themselves and the game by being challenged.

The following challenges start from the simplest forms of targets for the novice, up to much more in-depth drills to ensure even the 1st XI opener is striving to achieve something every session.

PRO TIP

Marcus Trescothick

"Every time I bat in the nets I have a specific purpose or goal of what I'm trying to achieve. Having markers or targets signifying gaps in the field is a great way of making the practice more game-specific and gives you the ability to gauge success."

BATSMEN TARGETS
Simple target games:

NOVICE
Challenge 1 – how many balls in a row can you either hit successfully, or leave (without getting bowled!), before you play and miss. Ball hitting pads counts as a play and miss.

COACHING TIP
Remind your players how important it is to watch the ball! Sometimes even experienced players forget to do it!

Challenge 2 – can you hit a set number of balls in a row (for example 6, or 12) along the floor, either defending or attacking.

COACHING TIP
One of the reasons that players are hitting the ball in the air when they don't mean to is because they are playing it too early. In order to get them to wait for the ball, get them to see if they can make the ball bounce as high as it can after they have hit it. This will make them hit it down.

NET PRACTICE – BATSMEN

PRO TIP

Dimitri Mascarenhas – "In order to hit the ball hard and to hit sixes – I have to practise my skills during training sessions. I try to maintain a solid base with two feet planted on the ground throughout the swing of the bat, and watch the ball as closely as I can to make sure I get a good contact. I swing hard through the line of the ball but try not to lose my 'body shape' as I'm making contact. Smashing sixes has got to be one of the most enjoyable parts of cricket!"

Challenge 3 – can you hit every ball bowled at you as hard as you can, regardless of line and length. How many balls in a row can you do this for without missing or mis-hitting a ball.

COACHING TIP

Hitting the ball hard is one of the best feelings in the game! In order to do so, you must keep your eyes on the ball, and try to get the blade of the bat travelling through the line of the ball. Then just keep practising!

Challenge 4 – can you hit every ball bowled at you as softly as possible. See just how much pace you can take off the ball. Try setting out an area in which the player is trying to make the ball stop.

COACHING TIP

Throughout these challenges, let the bowlers be aware of what the batsmen are trying to achieve, and see how they respond as well.

NET PRACTICE – BATSMEN

INTERMEDIATE

Challenge 1 – players must alternate hitting the ball into the off-side, or the leg-side no matter where the ball is bowled. In this way they must use their feet and body to manipulate the ball. Set a target of how many times they can do it successfully in a row.

COACHING TIP

Don't let the bowlers know what the batsmen are trying to do on this drill. Just let them know it's a one-day game practice and let them respond according to how the batsmen are playing.

Challenge 2 – players must hit alternate balls along the floor, and then in the air. Use of footwork and body position will aid them in this task.

COACHING TIP

Remind the players that to hit the ball on the ground they must strike it LATE, and to hit the ball in the air they must take it EARLY.

COACHING TIP

Another tip when hitting the ball hard is for the player to have a solid base – ie two feet on the ground. This will allow the maximum transfer of power into the bat.

Challenge 3 – players must hit alternate balls as HARD as they can (either in the air or along ground), and as SOFTLY as they can.

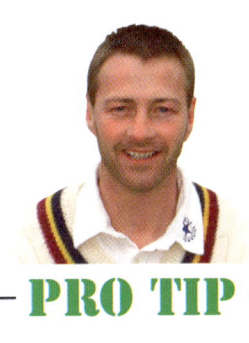

PRO TIP

Graeme Fowler – "When playing against fast bowlers I always felt that my pad was my friend, however when playing against spin I felt that it was my enemy. The way to combat this issue was to play with the bat in front of the pad against spinners, which means taking a smaller step towards the ball and getting your head and hands advanced of the front leg – yet staying balanced. This takes practice to make sure you are in a good position to play the ball."

Challenge 4 – set up two sets of stumps next to each other (see picture). Batsman must defend both sets of stumps whilst batting. How many balls can they survive?

NET PRACTICE – BATSMEN

Set up target areas in the nets using pairs of markers of the same colour – these can simulate gaps in the field for picking up singles or boundaries

ADVANCED
Challenge 1 – how many balls out of a set number bowled can the batsman manipulate into the gaps.

COACHING TIP
Ask player to think about how they could get the ball into the gap whilst still keeping the maximum amount of bat presented to the ball. You can get the ball safely behind square simply by playing it late.

Challenge 2 – can the batsman manipulate the balls into the gaps in a set order, i.e. work around the gaps in a clockwise fashion. Count how many times in a row they hit the gaps.

COACHING TIP
Discuss the role of the feet in trying to manipulate the gaps. Lining up the feet towards the target will give a better chance of success.

PRO TIP

Mark Ramprakash – "In order to improve as a batsman, you must train hard at your strengths, weaknesses and also try new things. You can't expect to have success with a shot in a game situation unless you've worked hard on it in practice."

Challenge 3 – set up a leg-side, or off-side dominated field, whereby there are three gaps on one side and only one gap on the other. See how successful batsmen are at manipulating to different sides of the wicket.

COACHING TIP

Set specific targets for the players to work towards. i.e. count how many times out of ten deliveries the batsman successfully finds the gap, so that they can be competitive with themselves and other team members

RUNNING NETS

You can make all of these challenges more game-based and interactive by having two players padded up at the same time. With each of the tasks, the batsman retains possession of the strike as long as they are successful in their task. So if they manage to hit five balls in a row without playing and missing, they keep the strike. As soon as they play and miss, the non-striker calls 'YES' and they sprint through for a single.

With the more advanced targets this can mean a good turnover of strike, and therefore a good running between the wickets fitness session as well.

VARIATION

Try turning things around so the batsman is trying to get off strike as quickly as possible, by running every time they complete the challenge successfully. Who can get off strike in the fewest balls possible? Or count how many balls each batsman faces individually and the lowest total wins.

NET PRACTICE – BATSMEN

BOWLER TARGETS
Simple target games for bowlers

NOVICE
Challenge 1 – score a point for every ball that bounces only once before the batsman. See how many points you can score in a set number of deliveries (e.g. 12)

Challenge 2 – draw a chalk line down middle stump. Score a point for every ball that bounces once regardless of line. Score two points if it also lands to the off-side of your chalk line, as long as it's not a wide.

Challenge 3 – score a point if you make the batsman leave, play and miss, or defend a delivery. See how many points you can score in a set number of deliveries? Have targets e.g. can you score 6 points in 12 deliveries. Adapt the challenge depending upon the skill level of the batsman.

COACHING TIP
By setting appropriate challenges for your bowlers, you can start to build their understanding of just what is needed to be a good bowler – i.e. control of where the ball is going.

NET PRACTICE – BOWLERS

INTERMEDIATE

Challenge 1 – set a target length either by chalk line, or by use of markers on the edge of the wicket. This should be a length which provokes indecision in the batsman as to whether to play forward or back. Player scores a point every time ball lands in this area. Count points and set targets of points per number of deliveries.

Challenge 2 – as per challenge 1, although also rate the shot that the batsman has to play into either attacking shot (zero extra points), defensive shot (1 extra point) or play and miss/leave (2 extra points). Bowler scores extra points only when ball pitches in target zone, and doesn't go down legside.

COACHING TIP

You can either tell the batsman the scoring system for these games or not. You might find that you get a different response from batsmen if they know what's going on so it's worth trying out both options.

PRO TIP

Shaun Udal – "In one-day cricket especially, I like to vary my pace and flight so that the batsman can't settle into a rhythm. In order to do this, I have used drills in practice trying to flight the ball over a certain height yet still land it in a target zone, and measured how well I can do this. I have also worked hard on developing a quicker delivery to try to catch the batsman off-guard!"

PRO TIP

Steve Kirby – "Whenever I'm practising either in the nets, or bowling to a 'keeper with no batsman, I always try to visualise the delivery that I'm trying to bowl. At the top of my run-up, I will focus on what I'm trying to do, how it will feel when it leaves my hand, and what the ball will look like as it's going down the pitch. This helps me to concentrate on exactly what I'm trying to achieve every single time I bowl a ball."

PRO TIP

Graeme Swann – "As a spinner I have to work extra hard on my accuracy, and this comes through commitment to practice. I have spent hours bowling at cones and targets – as well as batsmen – so that I'm confident I can land the ball in a good area as often as possible, even against the best players in the world! I really enjoy competition – so to have challenges in training makes it even better for me."

NET PRACTICE – BOWLERS

ADVANCED

Challenge 1 – highlight two areas that the bowlers are going to work on during the session, eg length balls and yorkers. Set markers or chalk lines on the wicket to signify exactly where these target zones are (see diagram). Players score a point every time they pitch the ball in a target zone.

Challenge 2 – highlight three areas as above; 'length', yorkers and bouncers, using markers or chalk lines. Set bowlers a pre-determined target set of six deliveries, e.g length, length, yorker, length, length, bouncer. Mark the players on their accuracy of being able to change their length according to the pre-set pattern. Set up a white-board with a chart on it so that the players have to rate each delivery and can add up success rate at the end.

	OVER 1	OVER 2	OVER 3
Ball 1	Length	Length	Bouncer
Ball 2	Length	Length	Yorker
Ball 3	Length	Yorker	Length
Ball 4	Yorker	Length	Bouncer
Ball 5	Length	Length	Yorker
Ball 6	Bouncer	Bouncer	Length

James Tomlinson – "I find it massively important to use targets in practice – they make me concentrate more and have definitely improved my accuracy and consistency. I generally place cones on a 'bouncer' length and a 'good' length and have even used a big bin in the past, placing it in the crease to simulate a batsman! These targets and the bin in particular help me firstly discover and then visualise where a good length really is."

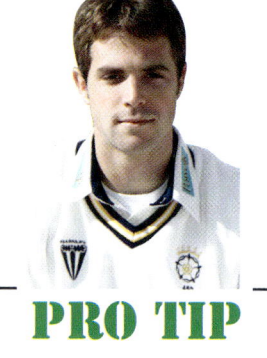

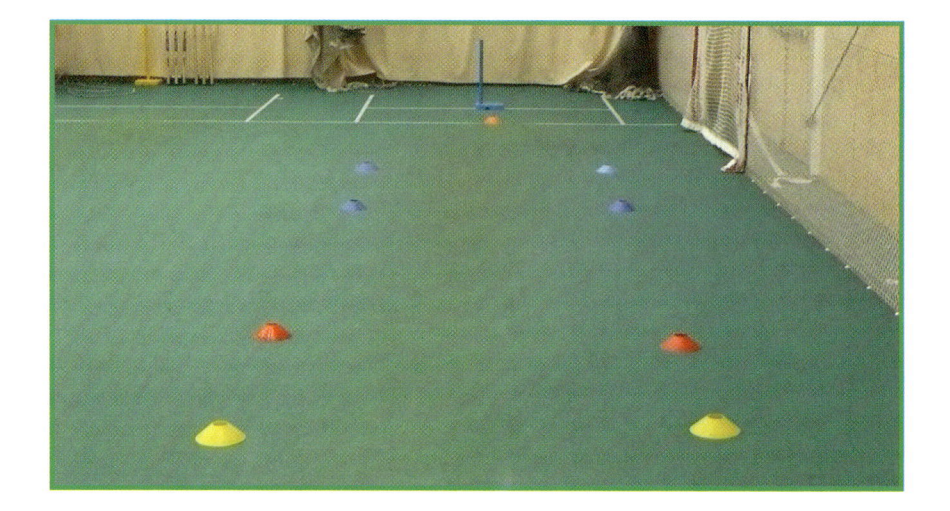

PRO TIP

PRO TIP

Chris Tremlett – "It is imperative that I know where I'm trying to bowl, and I have practised all of my different deliveries over and over in order to put pressure on a batsman. By challenging myself during practice I find it easier to step up to the match-situation, and that includes working on my stock ball and my slower deliveries….."

ADVANCED

Challenge 3 – practise variation balls! Discuss with each bowler their preferred method of bowling a slower ball, or for spinners an arm-ball or wrong-'un (googly). Ascertain what length they ideally want this delivery to land on, and set markers or chalk lines accordingly. Set targets of how many deliveries they can land in set areas per number of deliveries.

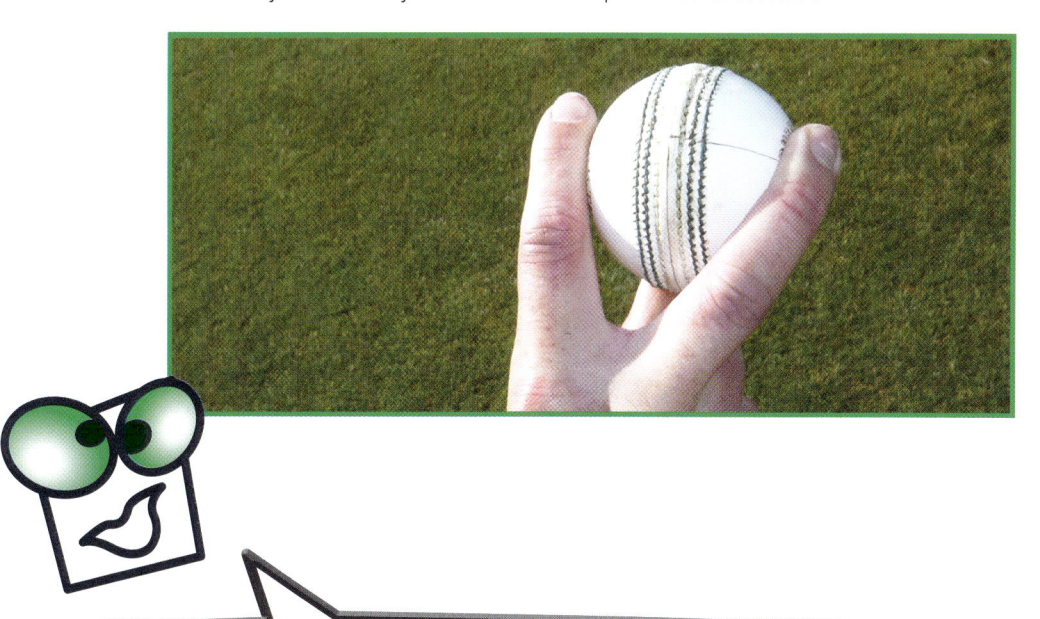

COACHING TIP

All of these bowler-specific practices can be performed either against the batsmen in the nets, or just in an empty net with the markers and targets on the wicket. To make it more challenging and interesting if there are no batsmen, set up games between the bowlers. Either pair bowlers up into even-skilled partners, who can score points against each other in a 1 vs. 1 situation, or have a group of bowlers all scoring points so that each session you have a winner.

Wicket-keeping

Wicket-keepers are often the forgotten men at club or squad training. However, they are a vital part of every team, and can set the tone in the field with their energy and enthusiasm, as well as tidy up any wild throws or wayward bowling. It's just as important for a wicket-keeper to have regular specific practice as it is for a bowler or batsman, and therefore they need to be practising their skills in every session possible, and not just bowling off-spinners in the nets to make up the numbers!

Over the next few pages, there are some simple drills you can use with your 'keepers to give them some quality practice, and make sure they are getting the attention that they deserve.

If you've got several 'keepers at a session then get them to work together, and they will learn off each other as they perform the different drills and discuss the techniques they use to catch different deliveries.

By setting up good quality and inspired training drills, they will start to develop their own techniques which will make them as effective as possible at catching as many balls as they can.

PRO TIP

James Foster – "The first thing I think is that I want to catch every single ball that is within my reach – at the end of the day this is what wicket-keeping is all about! In order to be in a position to achieve this goal, it is vital that I practise catching balls at all different heights, angles and trajectories. I love training with the guys – the fact that it's fun means I look forward to turning up every day!"

PRO TIP

Jon Batty – "As a wicket-keeper you must get your head and hands in a position which gives you the best chance of catching the ball. I work extremely hard on my skills at standing up to the wicket, and practise taking balls on the off-side, and down the leg-side with a shadow batsman regularly to put myself under the pressure of a game situation."

PRO TIP

Nic Pothas – "I catch balls of different sizes, shapes, weights and colours in training so that when it comes to a game I'm ready for absolutely anything. We use balls that are designed to swing in the air to simulate the ball moving after it has passed the batsman – which have been a great training aid. You just have to be innovative and think 'outside of the box' in order to get the most out of every session!"

WICKET-KEEPING

Basic catching drills

The most important aspect of wicket-keeping is catching the ball! Try these simple yet very effective drills that should be used in all wicket-keeping warm-ups to constantly reinforce hand-eye co-ordination as well as 'catching rhythm'.

Standing still – keeper stands still and feeder (either coach or other keeper) simply feeds ball straight at the keeper.

Press and Take – feeder now gets the ball going slightly wider than the keeper's hips on each side, so that the keeper has to take a small step with one leg towards line of ball, getting head and hands in line.

FEED VARIATIONS – perform the above drills firstly with ball reaching keeper on the full, then throw balls that land at least 2m in front of keeper and bounce up to about waist height. Finally put the keeper under more pressure by throwing half-volleys so they have to stay low and judge the pace off the surface.

COACHING TIP

In order to be an effective keeper you need to be able to catch the ball, so simply encourage your player to watch the ball and learn how to catch it in their own style!

One-handed drills

The quicker you can learn to catch efficiently with one hand, the better. This is both with your stronger and weaker hand. Work with a keeper partner and feed each other right hand to right hand, then left hand to left hand. Work on different heights, from ankle up to shoulder height.

Now try taking half-volleys with one hand. Start with the feeder throwing the ball on the half-volley between the keeper's legs, keeper takes it in turns to pick it up with right hand then left hand. Now try the same but feeding the ball outside the keeper's ankles, so they have to bend and reach for the pick-up.

VARIATIONS

Under-Over – start with underarm feeds, and progress to over arm.

Ball change – try using different sized and weighted balls during the one-handed drills to test for hand-eye coordination.

Hand-eye co-ordination

There are lots of ways to ask different questions of keepers in practice. Try starting your warm-up simply hitting the ball off a cricket bat at the keeper, but try using different types of ball. Start with a cricket ball, then use a tennis ball, then a golf ball, then an indoor ball. Try throwing two balls at the same time, but of different weights/sizes. These drills will help keepers learn how to catch absolutely anything, so that when they come to catching a cricket ball it will seem simple! Be innovative and inspired with the different types of ball you use!

WICKET-KEEPING

Movement drills: lateral movement

Try these simple yet very effective drills that should be used in all wicket-keeping warm-ups to constantly reinforce hand-eye co-ordination as well as 'catching rhythm'.

Set up – simply place two cones of different colours about 3-5m apart, depending upon the size of your keeper (smaller distance for shorter keeper).

Activity – keeper starts in the middle of the cones, and has to move laterally in response to a feed alternating between the left and right cones. Feeder waits for keeper to get back into starting position in middle of cones before next feed.

VARIATIONS

Bounce feed – the same drill as above but feed overarm with the ball bouncing before it gets to the keeper. This simulates taking a wide delivery.

Touch and back – an alternative way of feeding yet still getting lateral movement is to call a marker (ie. 'Left' or 'Right'), which the keeper must move laterally towards, and touch with hand, and feed comes back into the middle of the cones. In this way the feeder only has to feed straight down the middle each time, yet the keeper is moving left and right.

One-handed – Keeper has to take ball with one hand after moving laterally towards the cone.

Wrong hand – keeper has to touch the cone as called by the feeder, but this time they have to move quick enough to get their whole body past the feed in the middle and catch in the hand closest to the cone they have just touched.

Zig-zag pick-up

Set-up – cones are placed in two lines approximately 3m apart, forming a zig-zag track (see diagram). Cricket balls are placed on every cone down one side of the track.

Activity – keepers have to pick up each ball, and move laterally to place it on the next available cone, before repeating all the way down the zig-zag.

VARIATIONS

Team game – if you have several keepers they can all work on this drill at the same time. Have keepers lined up at each end of the zig-zag track so that when the first keeper puts down the final ball, the keeper from the far end starts with the first pick-up, returning the balls to their original positions.

Speed up – start with the keepers going through slowly and deliberately, and after each completed run through the zig-zag, they have to go through a step quicker next time. This continues until they make a mistake in either picking the ball up or putting it on the cone. Make it competitive with forfeits for mistakes.

Chase – start with your keepers lined up at one end. First keeper starts, and when they are picking up the second ball, the second keeper is released and tries to chase them. You can make the zig-zag as long as you like, and have a chase with as many keepers as you want.

WICKET-KEEPING

Coloured rows

Set-up – have six cones set out, three at the front (all different colours) and three at the back (all different colours). You can have either one or two feeders depending on how many people are training (see diagram).

Activity – keeper starts on front middle cone. Feeder shouts random colour of a cone on the back row, and keeper moves back to touch it. Just as back row cone is touched, feeder calls colour of cone on the front row, and keeper moves towards this one. Just as keeper reaches the front cone the feeder provides an underarm throw for keeper to get set for and catch. Repeat this five or six times, calling a back cone, then a front cone, then a catch. Encourage to move in wicket-keeper style – i.e. lateral movements as much as possible.

VARIATIONS

Colourchange – try letting the players have a go at the drill a couple of times, and then change the cones around so that different colours are in different positions. This will keep them on their toes and provide more to think about!

Numbers – to provide a different challenge for the keeper, try giving each cone a number rather than a colour, and keep to the same method as above. This will provide a different stimulus for the player to respond to, and give them a bit of fun if you can catch them out!

Row change – be inspired with your marker lay-out, it doesn't have to be two rows of three cones, try adding another cone or two to each row, or maybe having three rows of cones. Different lay-outs will keep the players moving different distances – which will aid the learning process of moving and catching.

WICKET-KEEPING

Standing up drills

The hardest part of wicket-keeping is standing up to the wicket, either to spinners or to seam bowlers. The only way to get better at this tough skill, is to practise it, and enjoy the challenges so that you look forward to showing off your skills. Getting your keeper used to practising standing up will help them enormously and give them confidence when going into a game.

Off side, leg side

Set-up – a set of stumps and your wicket keeper.

Start off feeding outside the off-stump with easy length balls bouncing up to about waist height. If keeper is taking these regularly and well, start making the length fuller, until they are nearly half-volleys. See how many takes in a row the keeper can complete. Set targets and keep score. Then start feeding all different lengths, and again challenge how many times your keeper can take the ball in a row.

Perform the same drill, but now with the keeper setting themselves up outside the off-stump, and the feed going down the legside.

Once the keeper is proficient at taking balls down the leg-side, now set a new challenge, with your feed either going off-side OR leg-side.

Shadowing

Set-up – You need at least two keepers, or a willing volunteer armed with a bat, and a set of stumps. One of the reasons that standing up to the stumps is so hard, is because of the batsman getting in the line of view, and making the keeper unsure whether the ball will come through to them or not. So it's really important that keepers get a chance to practise with a batsman in front of them, and an effective way of doing this is through 'shadowing'. This is where a batsman stands in position and plays realistic cricket shots but deliberately misses the ball, allowing the keeper to practise having a bat waving around in front of them. Start off with balls outside the off-stump, and begin to vary the length.

Now for the hard part, feeding down the leg-side. Make sure that the batsman or shadower knows that you are feeding leg-side deliveries, as they will need to move out of the way if the ball is in line to hit them! This is a really important part of wicket-keeping and the earlier keepers can start practising this the better they will become, but it's never too late to start! Throw the ball so that it bounces once and goes down the legside by about a metre. Once the keeper gets used to catching these you can start to vary the line and length of the throw.

VARIATION

If you can't get someone to 'shadow' for you, be inspired as to what else to use to get in the line of sight of the batsman. Try using a large wheely-bin if one is available, or even make your own shadow batsman out of a large bit of card attached to a couple of stumps! Be inventive and make the sessions enjoyable and effective.

WICKET-KEEPING

Wimbledon drill

Set-up – if you have a tennis racquet and some tennis balls, bring these along to keeping practice, as well as a set of stumps. Keepers should just wear their inner gloves, and not main gloves for these drills.

Have your keeper in normal position for standing up to the stumps, but feed by hitting the ball rather than throwing it. This will allow you to increase the velocity of your speed – if you have the required tennis skills!

VARIATION
Try this also with a shadower if you are confident that they aren't in danger from your first serve!

Snicking drills

Set-up – you need a standard thin plastic cone, a batting glove, and at least two keepers.

The keeper sets up in normal style for standing up. Feeder is about 4-5m away and on one knee, batsman has batting glove on hand, holding the plastic cone. Feeder provides a firm underarm throw to reach the keeper at about waist height on the full, and the batsman tries to get a small nick on the ball with the edge of the cone as the ball passes them (This requires a bit of skill on the batsman's part!).

This is a great drill for providing practice of thin nicks when standing up to the stumps, and teaches the keeper to stay relaxed and keep their hands in a good position behind the ball, even when something is moving at a fast pace.

Do this for both right and left-handed batsmen.

INSPIRED CRICKET
PRACTISE LIKE THE PROS

Hopefully the drills and games in this manual will help you put on fun and challenging sessions for all of your players.

Remember, there is no limit to what you can do, just be INSPIRED!

Please visit the website for further info at www.inspiredcricket.com

INDEX

DRILL INDEX

Warm ups:

American Football Drill	22
Bases	16
The Chase	26
Cricket-Football	28
Cross-over Grid	18
Dynamic Shuttles	24
Four-goal Fandango	30
In the Square	14
Keep Ball	27
Ladder Circuit	20
Military Lap	21
Vortex/Frisbee	29

Agility Drills:

Catch-2	34
Fielding Star	33
Ladder work 1	36
Ladder Work 2	38
The Pod	35

Throwing Drills:

Directs Hits	41
Dynamic Run Saving	42
Four Stations Four Jobs	44
The Grid	46
Fielding Races 1	49
Fielding Races 2	50
Fielding Races 3	51
Quickfire Stump-hitting	48

Catching Drills:

American Football Catching	60
Baseball Racing Game	59
Goaltending	64
Hand-Eye Co-Ordination	56
Pairs High Catching	62
Quadrangle Quick Hands	58
Relay Catching	66
The Snake	54
Weakest Link Catching	61

Net Challenges:

Batting – Novice	70
Batting – Intermediate	72
Batting – Advanced	74
Bowlers – Novice	78
Bowlers – Intermediate	79
Bowlers – Advanced	80
Running nets	76

Wicket-Keeping:

Basic Catching Drills	84
Coloured Rows	89
Lateral Movement	86
One-Handed Drills	85
Off-Side Leg-Side	90
Shadowing	91
Snicking Drills	93
Wimbledon Drills	92
Zig-Zag Pick-up	88

QUOTE INDEX

Batty, Jon	83
Foster, James	83
Fowler, Graeme	73
Harvey, Ian	32
Kirby, Steve	79
Langer, Justin	13
Mascarenhas, Dimi	71
Maynard, Matthew	21
Pietersen, Kevin	11
Pothas, Nic	83
Ramprakash, Mark	75
Swann, Graeme	79
Tremlett, Chris	81
Trescothick, Marcus	69
Tomlinson, James	80
Udal, Shaun	79

INSPIRED CRICKET

PRACTISE LIKE THE PROS